UNVEILING THE EXTRAORDINARY JOURNEY OF CHRIS EVANS

A Tale of Courage, Compassion, and the Man
Behind the Captain America Legacy.

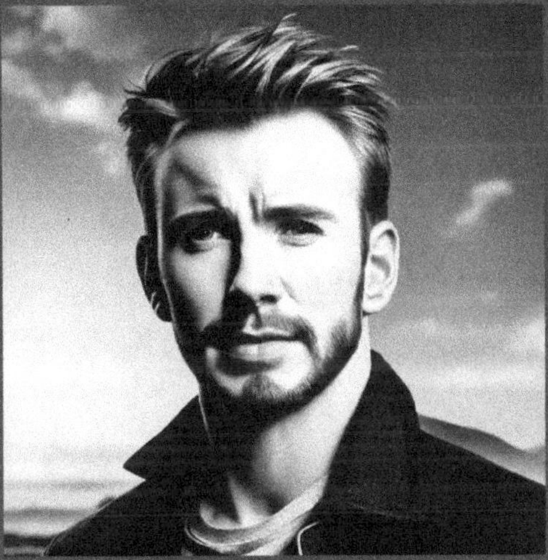

Rodney G. Wooten

Unveiling the Extraordinary Journey of Chris Evans

A Tale of Courage, Compassion, and the Man Behind the Captain America Legacy.

By

Rodney G. Wooten

Table of content

Introduction
Chapter one
   A Modest Start
   Becoming Captain America
      Glimpses into the private life and experiences of Chris Evans.
Chapter two
   Action, camera, lights!
    Marvel's Legacy
   The Hero's Heart
Chapter three
   Love and Relationships
   Obstacles and Achievements
   Chris Evans Versatility in movie industry
Chapter four
    Chris Evans worked and appeared with co-stars
   The Aftereffects of a Superhuman
   Moral lessons from the life of Chris Evans
   Summary

Introduction

Welcome to the once-in-a-lifetime trip!
Enter the enthralling realm of story with a book titled "**Unveiling the Extraordinary Journey of Chris Evans**" where the remarkable story of Hollywood's most beloved superhero leaps off the pages in this book. Prepare to go beyond the flash and sparkle to discover the true nature of the guy who plays the legendary parts.

Come along as we explore Chris Evans's wild journey to popularity, from the early hardships that molded him to the lofty ascent to become the renowned Captain America. This is an intimate look into the highs, lows, and everything in between—it's more than simply a biography.

Learn about the superhero-sized heart that characterizes Chris Evans, the power of self-discovery, and the lessons of perseverance. Have you ever wondered what happens behind those recognizable suits and shields? As we lift the layers and uncover the true, real, and very relatable human being, be ready to be astounded. But the lessons are more important than the glamor. Beyond the Shield is a manual for overcoming obstacles in life that places a strong emphasis on tenacity, development as a person, and the heroic effects of social duty. It's an encouragement to embrace your path and a celebration of honesty.

So have a seat, my dear reader! This book offers tears, humor, and a ton of inspiration, regardless of whether you're a devoted fan or merely inquiring about the guy behind the superhero.

Chapter one

A Modest Start

Chris Evans's early life and upbringing influenced him.

Chris Evans, whose real name is Christopher Robert Evans, was born in Boston, Massachusetts, in the United States on June 13, 1981. His background and early years had a big influence on how captivating an actor he became.

Evans was raised in a close-knit family in the Massachusetts town of Sudbury. Evans's passion for the arts was instilled in him at an early age by his mother, Lisa Capuano, who was the creative director of the Concord Youth Theater. G. Robert Evans III, his father, was a dentist. Chris has a brother named Scott and two sisters named Carly and Shanna. It was partly the supportive atmosphere of the family that fueled his early acting interest.

Evans's interest in performing arts developed when he was a student at Lincoln-Sudbury Regional High School in his early years. He demonstrated his innate aptitude and theatrical presence by taking part in school musicals and plays. Evans discovered acting to be his genuine calling and followed it with tenacity despite having a strong academic background.

Chris Evans began his acting career in the late 1990s, doing television shows such as "Opposite Sex" and "Boston Public." In the 2001 comedy "Not Another Teen Movie," he made his debut and showcased his comic skills. But what brought him to the attention of the general public was his performance as Johnny Storm/Human Torch in Marvel's "Fantastic Four" (2005) and its follow-up.

Evans had difficulties making the shift from youthful romantic parts to ones that were more diversified and serious. He proved to be versatile and deep in movies like "Sunshine" (2007) and

"Street Kings" (2008), despite the initial mistrust. When he agreed to play the legendary Captain America/Steve Rogers role in the Marvel Cinematic Universe (MCU), his career took a dramatic change.

Evans was well praised for his depiction of Captain America, embodying the emblem of courage. Audiences were moved by his physical and emotional commitment to the part, which cemented his place as one of Hollywood's top actors. Beyond his success on film, Evans addressed social concerns and promoted causes near and dear to his heart using his platform.

Chris Evans's success throughout his career has been attributed to his early exposure to the arts and his supportive familial environment. His rise from small-town theater roles to being one of the most well-known performers globally is a testament to his skill, tenacity, and sincere love of telling stories. Without question, Chris Evans' early experiences helped to build him into the multifaceted

Chris Evans has received recognition for his charity contributions and philanthropic endeavors in addition to his acting abilities. Evans was raised in a household that valued community and the arts, and as a result, he felt a strong sense of duty to give back.

Evans's commitment to children's hospitals and his engagement in philanthropic work are two noteworthy aspects of his character. He has supported charities such as Christopher's Haven, a nonprofit that houses families whose children are receiving cancer treatment. Evans has continuously raised money and awareness for these causes by using his platform, which demonstrates his sincere desire to have a beneficial influence outside of the entertainment business.

Evans is not just a kind man but also a strong advocate for social and political causes. His readiness to voice opinions on issues like racial injustice, climate warming, and LGBTQ+ rights demonstrates his dedication to utilizing his platform to bring about constructive change. Undoubtedly, his childhood, where conversations concerning the arts often touched on more general societal concerns, had an impact on his social consciousness.

Throughout his career in Hollywood, Chris Evans has grown from a young actor navigating the difficulties of the business to an accomplished performer and supporter of constructive change. His ability to strike a balance between big-budget parts and more intimate, character-driven roles showcases both his breadth as an actor and his dedication to creating compelling stories.

Evans has made insinuations about leaving acting to pursue other ventures, but there is no denying his influence on popular culture and film. His early years and upbringing, which were characterized by exposure to the arts and a loving family, prepared him for a career in film and television.

In addition to his legendary on-screen personas, Chris Evans' legacy will be shaped by his sincere desire to change the world while he navigates the ever-changing entertainment industry. His destiny is still shaped by the beliefs that were ingrained in him throughout his early years.

Amidst his success in Hollywood, Chris Evans has also dabbled in directing, exhibiting an additional aspect of his creative ability. This change is a reflection of his want to make a more substantial contribution to the filmmaking process. Evans was able to further establish his name in the business and experiment with a new narrative technique with his directing debut, "Before We Go" (2014).

Outside of the movie industry's flash and glitter, Chris Evans has been open about his battles with worry and self-doubt. By sharing these personal struggles with his followers, he has won their affection and given a human face to the legendary Hollywood star character. In addition to helping to lessen the stigma associated with mental health, this openness establishes a more intimate connection with viewers.

The public has also been interested in Chris Evans' love life, and he has handled the limelight with a degree of solitude that differs from the severe scrutiny that celebrities often experience. His cautious attitude to his private life is a reflection of his dedication to upholding normality and safeguarding people who are dear to him.

Chris Evans continues to be a major player in the entertainment industry as he takes on a variety of roles and projects. In addition to his devotion to charity and social concerns, his ability to strike a balance between indie films and blockbuster franchises highlights his commitment to authenticity and purpose in both his personal and professional lives.

Chris Evans' early life and upbringing, in short, prepared him for a profession characterized by adaptability, resiliency, and a strong sense of duty. From a budding performer in neighborhood theater to a well-known celebrity, he has succeeded in upholding his moral principles and making a lasting impression on the entertainment world. Chris Evans' brilliance, genuineness, and dedication to changing the world will undoubtedly continue to captivate fans as the next chapters of his career take shape, both on and off-screen.

Chris Evans is ready to take on new chances and challenges in the future that fit with his developing creative vision. Evans is dedicated to a vibrant and meaningful profession, whether it means pushing the boundaries of his art, advocating for social concerns, or continuing his investigation of directing.

His standing as a cinematic legend has been cemented by the lasting impact he leaves in the Marvel Cinematic Universe as Captain America. Evans, meanwhile, has said that he consciously seeks roles that highlight his breadth as an actor to avoid being put into stereotypes. This tendency to broaden his repertoire shows a continued commitment to personal development in addition to a devotion to his trade.

Chris Evans often stresses in public appearances and interviews the value of being honest and true to oneself in the face of pressure from the entertainment industry. Because of his genuineness, skill, and relatability, he has gained a large following of people all over the world who value not just the characters he plays but also the real guy behind the parts.

Beyond the screen, Chris Evans continues to play a significant role in the entertainment industry's ongoing evolution. His path serves as a reminder of the ideals that may lead to a successful and rewarding profession as well as a source of inspiration for the next generation of actors and filmmakers. His effect on them is evident.

Although the particulars of Chris Evans' next endeavors are yet unknown, his dedication to social activism, storytelling, and honesty will likely continue to influence his tale. Chris Evans is a living example of the lasting power of skill, resiliency, and a sincere connection with the work and the audience as he navigates the ever-shifting world of celebrity and creation.

Becoming Captain America

The audition, transformation, and the impact of portraying the iconic superhero.

Chris Evans' journey to becoming Captain America was a multi-faceted process that involved auditions, physical transformations, and the profound impact of embodying such an iconic superhero.

1. **The Audition Process:** The casting of Captain America for the Marvel Cinematic Universe (MCU) was a meticulous process, with several actors vying for the role. Initially, Chris Evans hesitated to accept the offer, concerned about the long-term commitment and the potential impact on his personal life. However, after conversations with friends and fellow actors, he reconsidered, recognizing the significance of portraying a character as emblematic as Captain America. Evans underwent a series of

auditions, showcasing not only his acting prowess but also his understanding of the character's depth and moral complexity. His ability to convey the vulnerability beneath Captain America's stoic exterior impressed both the casting directors and Marvel Studios.

2. **Physical Transformation:** Taking on the role of Captain America required a significant physical transformation. Evans underwent a rigorous workout regimen, working closely with trainers to build the muscular physique synonymous with the superhero. The commitment to the physical demands of the role showcased Evans' dedication to authenticity and his willingness to fully inhabit the character. Beyond the physical aspects, Evans also delved into the psychological nuances of Captain America. He embraced the responsibility of portraying a symbol of heroism and integrity, recognizing the character's impact on audiences,

especially younger viewers who looked up to superheroes as role models.

3. **Impact and Legacy:** Portraying Captain America had a profound impact on Chris Evans both personally and professionally. The role catapulted him to international fame and established him as a cornerstone of the MCU. Beyond the box office success, Evans' portrayal resonated with audiences, earning him widespread acclaim for bringing depth and humanity to the superhero genre. Captain America became a cultural icon under Evans' stewardship, evolving from a patriotic symbol to a complex and relatable character. The trilogy of Captain America films— "The First Avenger," "The Winter Soldier," and "Civil War"— showcased Evans' range as an actor and contributed to the critical and commercial success of the MCU. The legacy of Chris Evans as Captain America extends beyond the screen. His dedication to the role, coupled

with his off-screen charisma, solidified him as a beloved figure in popular culture. Evans' portrayal of Captain America not only left an indelible mark on the MCU but also shaped the broader conversation about the significance of superheroes in contemporary storytelling. In retrospect, Chris Evans' journey to becoming Captain America was more than a career milestone; it was a transformative experience that highlighted his commitment to his craft and the enduring impact of portraying an iconic superhero.

4. **Evolution of the Character:** As Chris Evans continued to portray Captain America across multiple films in the MCU, the character underwent significant growth and evolution. From his origin story in "The First Avenger" to the emotionally charged events in "Endgame," Evans masterfully navigated the complexities of Captain America's journey. The character's internal struggles,

moral dilemmas, and the weight of leadership became central themes in Evans' portrayal. Captain America wasn't just a superhuman figure; he was a symbol of resilience, sacrifice, and unwavering principles. Evans infused the character with a sense of vulnerability and humanity that resonated with audiences, transcending the traditional superhero archetype.

5. **Impact on Pop Culture:** Chris Evans' embodiment of Captain America became a cultural touchstone. The character's shield, iconic costume, and Evans' charismatic portrayal contributed to a resurgence of interest in superhero narratives. Captain America's catchphrase "I can do this all day" became a rallying cry for determination and courage. The impact extended beyond the films themselves, with Captain America emerging as a symbol of hope and inspiration in a world facing real-world

challenges. Evans, both on and off-screen, embraced the responsibility that came with portraying such an influential character, using his platform to address social issues and engage with fans on a personal level.

6. **Emotional Farewell:** Chris Evans' journey as Captain America reached an emotional climax in "Avengers: Endgame." The film marked the end of an era for the MCU and provided a fitting conclusion to Captain America's story arc. Evans delivered a poignant and heartfelt performance, encapsulating the character's legacy and the actor's farewell to the role. Evans' decision to hang up the shield was met with a mix of emotions from fans, further highlighting the profound impact of his portrayal. The legacy of Captain America lived on, but it was clear that Evans had left an indelible mark on the character, contributing to the emotional

resonance of the MCU's overarching narrative.

7. **Post-Captain America Career:** Following his tenure as Captain America, Chris Evans continued to diversify his career with projects like "Knives Out" and "Defending Jacob." This post-Captain America phase showcased Evans' versatility as an actor, proving that he could seamlessly transition from the superhero genre to nuanced and character-driven roles. In summary, Chris Evans' journey as Captain America was a transformative experience that not only elevated the character to iconic status but also solidified Evans as a respected and versatile actor. His impact on pop culture, coupled with the emotional depth he brought to the role, ensures that his portrayal of Captain America remains etched in the annals of cinematic history.

8. **Beyond the Shield:** Exploring Diverse Roles Chris Evans, post his iconic portrayal of Captain America, embarked on a deliberate journey to explore diverse roles that showcased the breadth of his acting abilities. This transition demonstrated his commitment to avoiding type casting and challenging himself with a range of characters. In "Knives Out" (2019), Evans embraced a sharp departure from the superhero genre, portraying Ransom Drysdale, a wealthy and cunning character in a murder mystery ensemble. His charismatic and unpredictable performance garnered critical acclaim, affirming his capability to excel in roles outside the realm of superheroes. "Defending Jacob" (2020), an Apple TV+ series, further underscored Evans' versatility. Here, he portrayed a father grappling with complex moral and emotional dilemmas as his family becomes entangled in a legal investigation. The series showcased

Evans' ability to navigate the intricacies of a dramatic, character-driven narrative on the small screen.

9. **Exploring Directorial Ventures:** In addition to his acting endeavors, Chris Evans extended his creative pursuits to the director's chair. "Before We Go" (2014), his directorial debut, allowed him to not only explore a different facet of storytelling but also revealed his interest in narratives centered on human connections and relationships. As Evans continues to navigate his post-Captain America career, there is anticipation surrounding his feature directorial projects and how he will further shape the landscape of storytelling both in front of and behind the camera.

10. **Social Advocacy and Philanthropy:** Beyond the world of entertainment, Chris Evans maintained his commitment to social advocacy and philanthropy. He

continued to use his platform to address important issues, whether it be promoting civic engagement, raising awareness about climate change, or advocating for social justice causes. Evans' active engagement with social and environmental issues showcased a desire to leverage his influence for positive change, aligning with the real-world values he brought to the portrayal of Captain America.

11. **Legacy and Impact:** Chris Evans' legacy extends far beyond the characters he portrayed on screen. His journey from a talented actor in local theater to a global superstar showcased not only his acting prowess but also his resilience, authenticity, and dedication to making a positive impact in various spheres. As he forges ahead in his career, fans and critics alike eagerly anticipate the next chapters in the Chris Evans story. Whether in front of the camera, behind it, or through his philanthropic efforts, one thing remains

certain: Chris Evans will continue to shape the entertainment industry and beyond with his talent, charisma, and unwavering commitment to meaningful storytelling and positive change.

Glimpses into the private life and experiences of Chris Evans.

Widely known for his legendary performance as Captain America in the Marvel Cinematic Universe, Chris Evans has developed an appealing and charismatic persona that exudes charm and an authentic love of life, both on and off-screen. Numerous life events that have molded Evans into the adored actor and person he is today have contributed to his rise to fame.

Evans is well-known off-screen for his commitment to social causes and philanthropy. He has made a concerted effort to encourage citizens to take part in civic engagement and the democratic process. To promote informed and involved citizens, Evans co-founded the nonpartisan website "A Starting Point," which offers succinct and objective information about political issues.

Beyond his advocacy work, Evans has been open about his battles with anxiety and how the demands of celebrity have affected him. He has discussed his early career struggles candidly in interviews, including concerns about his capacity to handle the scope of big-budget roles. Fans have responded well to his candor when he talks about mental health concerns, and this has fueled the ongoing discussion about mental health in the entertainment industry.

The passion that Chris Evans has for the arts is also evident in his off-screen life. He has shown a desire to broaden his creative horizons and has dabbled in directing with the film "Before We Go" in addition to acting. His involvement in different projects both in front of and behind the camera demonstrates his commitment to artistic expression as well as his nuanced storytelling style.

More importantly, Evans is renowned for upholding tight bonds with his loved ones and friends. Even though he's on the A-list, he frequently stresses the value of remaining authentic and grounded. Through his interactions with followers on social media, where he shares hilarious and lighter moments, fans have been able to get a taste of his playful and humorous side.

In terms of partnerships, Evans has been largely quiet, although his high-profile romances and dating life have sometimes made headlines. However, he remains protective of his personal space and enjoys a degree of solitude among the attention that comes with celebrity.

A guy who goes beyond his superhero identity is shown in Chris Evans' off-screen life, where he demonstrates a love of the arts, a candor about personal challenges, and a dedication to social concerns. As he continues to navigate the entertainment world, his admirers anxiously await the next chapters in his career and the insights he will continue to provide into his diverse life.

In recent years, Chris Evans has expanded his career by taking on jobs that push him as an actor and add to the cinematic world. His performances in films like "Knives Out" have proved his flexibility and ability to handle parts beyond the superhero genre.

Evans has dedicated himself to several philanthropic endeavors in addition to the flash and glamor of Hollywood. He has been a passionate champion of environmental problems and has utilized his position to raise awareness about climate change. His interest in philanthropy extends to sponsoring groups that concentrate on problems such as education, children's health, and social justice.

In 2020, Chris Evans found himself in the center of an unanticipated social media controversy after he mistakenly uploaded a private picture on his Instagram story. Instead of shying away from the occurrence, Evans took the occasion to encourage civic involvement, pushing people to vote while light-heartedly addressing the problem. The event demonstrated his ability to face hardship with elegance and humor, endearing him even more to his followers.

Despite his celebrity, Evans has managed to establish a true relationship with his audience. Whether it's via sincere interviews, engaging social media postings, or his encounters at fan gatherings, he continually expresses thanks for the love he gets and humility that connects with supporters worldwide.

Looking ahead, Chris Evans' followers anxiously await his next ventures and the continuous influence he will have both on and off the screen. As he navigates the ever-evolving terrain of Hollywood, one can expect him to bring the same amount of devotion, honesty, and enthusiasm to every effort, confirming his reputation not only as a superhero on-screen but as a versatile and important man in the world of entertainment.

In recent years, Chris Evans has continued to harness his platform for important storytelling. As a result of his involvement, the miniseries "Defending Jacob" presented a sophisticated examination of the challenges faced by parents and the details of the judicial system. He has shown flexibility in a sector that is undergoing fast change with this foray into the streaming services market.

Evans has never wavered in his support of social concerns. He often uses his position of power to solve social concerns, sponsoring programs that serve impoverished areas and fighting for equal rights. He adds to the continuing discussion about social advancement and development by using his famous profile to draw attention to these crucial talks.

The actor has a passion for narrative that goes beyond classic TV and movies. Entering the realm of audiobooks, he has contributed his voice to narrate both fiction and non-fiction volumes. Through this endeavor, he not only demonstrates his love of writing but also offers readers a unique method to engage with stories told in his own style.

Despite his successful Hollywood career, Chris Evans maintains a grounded demeanor, highlighting the importance of preserving authenticity in a superficiality-prone field. His open, approachable demeanor in interviews and public settings helps him establish a stronger bond with his listeners.

Evans's admirers eagerly await each new endeavor as he continues to grow as a professional. Whether he's portraying complicated characters in smaller shows or wearing the recognizable Captain America shield, he never fails to wow audiences. With an unwavering influence on the entertainment business and the wider cultural environment, Chris Evans' off-screen story, which is molded by charity, personal development, and a dedication to making a good effect, is still being told.

Chris Evans has welcomed the chance to work with other creatives in addition to his contributions to the entertainment sector. His participation in the virtual reading program "All In Challenge," in which well-known people donated unique experiences to generate money for COVID-19 aid, is a prime example of his commitment to changing the world under difficult circumstances.

To further solidify his status as a versatile musician, Evans has also dabbled in producing. He actively crafts stories and projects that speak to him personally by exploring the behind-the-scenes facets of filmmaking. The intention behind this production endeavor is to impact storytelling on a larger scale and aid in the development of varied and captivating material.

Evans has shown a love of physical fitness outside of his professional endeavors, often posting sneak peeks of his training regimens on social media. His promotion for complete well-being, which emphasizes the significance of both physical and mental health, is consistent with his commitment to maintaining a healthy lifestyle.

Chris Evans manages his public image while staying true to himself, making him a mysterious figure as he makes his way through the ever-changing world of celebrity. In addition to his charitable work and artistic interests, his capacity to relate to viewers on a human level further cedes his standing as a long-lasting cultural influencer rather than merely a Hollywood celebrity. Followers excitedly anticipate the next chapters in Chris Evans' life, both on and off screen, as he leaves his imprint on the entertainment business and beyond.

Chapter two

Action, camera, lights!

"The difficulties that Chris Evans faced while pursuing his acting career"

Chris Evans's journey reflects the competitive nature of Hollywood, where talent and resilience are crucial. Evans entered the acting world with determination, overcoming obstacles like auditions, rejections, and industry pressures. His success in iconic roles like Captain America is a testament to his ability to navigate the complexities of the entertainment industry.

Beyond the flash and glamor, Evans had to deal with the demands of public opinion and the difficulties of leading a balanced private life in the public eye. For actors such as him, juggling the demands of celebrity and privacy is a delicate dance. Moreover, the ever-changing nature of the business necessitates flexibility and ongoing skill development.

But Chris Evans has also emphasized the responsibility that comes with being a celebrity by using his platform for social causes. He has supported charitable endeavors and pushed for political participation, for example, demonstrating his dedication to having a positive influence outside of the movie industry.

Chris Evans is a living example of perseverance, adaptability, and the never-ending quest for greatness in the fast-paced world of acting.
While navigating the spotlight, Chris Evans has also embraced a variety of roles, defying stereotypes and demonstrating his versatility. The need for actors to break free from typecasting is another obstacle, but Evans's openness to trying out different genres is a testament to his commitment to the industry.

Chris Evans, like many others, has adjusted to these changes by taking part in projects that reach audiences through multiple mediums. In an era of rapid technological advancement, the industry itself has transformed, introducing new challenges and opportunities. Digital platforms and streaming services have altered the traditional landscape, impacting how actors approach their careers.

Despite the challenges, Evans' journey exemplifies the timeless appeal of telling stories through acting. As he keeps making contributions to the film industry, his experiences shed light on how the entertainment industry is changing and the perseverance needed to succeed in it.

As he continues his acting career, Chris Evans struggles to maintain his authenticity while fulfilling the expectations of the industry. Actors are often expected to project a certain image both on and off-screen, which can be intimidating. Evans has made a point of speaking out about the significance of remaining true to oneself in the face of external pressures.

The global nature of the film industry also brings with it cultural nuances and challenges; working with a diverse cast and crew necessitates a higher level of cultural sensitivity, which adds another level of complexity to the challenges actors face; Evans' dedication to promoting inclusivity and understanding is indicative of an awareness of the dynamic changes in the industry.

As Chris Evans leaves his imprint on the acting scene, his path serves as a captivating tale of tenacity, flexibility, and the everlasting pursuit of creative quality in the ever-evolving world of entertainment. Looking forward, the future offers new experiences and challenges.

Amid the constantly shifting terrain of Hollywood, Chris Evans has also embraced opportunities off-camera. His move into producing and directing shows his desire to add to storytelling from a different angle. Handling these complex roles calls for both business savvy and creative vision, as success in this field is increasingly dependent on one's capacity to wear many hats.

The introduction of social media has further changed the way actors interact with their audience. Chris Evans, like many of his colleagues, uses these platforms to communicate directly with fans, offer behind-the-scenes looks at his work, and support charitable causes. Nevertheless, this digital exposure also increases the difficulties associated with being scrutinized by the public and the necessity of maintaining a well-curated online presence.

The story of Chris Evans' ascent to fame and his experiences in the entertainment business enthrall viewers as he embarks on new chapters in his career. It provides a window into the complex web of obstacles, successes, and constant change in the entertainment industry.

Stories are no longer limited to print media in this day and age. Chris Evans delves into the ever-expanding world of content creation; podcasts, web series, and other novel formats enable him to engage audiences in novel ways and demonstrate the entertainment industry's transition to more varied and approachable forms of entertainment.

Furthermore, the global nature of content consumption necessitates an understanding of international markets and cultural nuances. Chris Evans, as a seasoned actor, embraces the opportunity to contribute to narratives that resonate with a wide spectrum of viewers, transcending geographical boundaries.

Chris Evans represents the flexibility needed in a field that is always changing as he breaks new ground in the entertainment industry. His journey is an example for aspiring actors and a tribute to the perseverance required to succeed in the complex world of light, camera, and action.

In the ever-evolving universe of entertainment, Chris Evans continues to be a light of originality and innovation. Collaborating with new talents and veteran industry leaders, he not only adds to the legacy of legendary characters but also defines the storylines of the future.

The challenges faced by actors like Evans extend beyond the set, delving into the realms of mental health awareness and self-care. The constant demand for perfection and the weight of public expectations underscores the importance of fostering a supportive environment within the industry.

As he embraces the dynamic nature of acting and the broader entertainment spectrum, Chris Evans stands at the intersection of tradition and innovation. His journey remains a testament to the enduring passion that fuels the world of acting, reminding us that behind every cinematic masterpiece is a story of determination, resilience, and the unwavering pursuit of artistic expression.

Looking forward, the trajectory of Chris Evans' career sparks anticipation for what lies ahead. The evolution of storytelling methods, the rise of immersive technologies, and the exploration of uncharted narratives open new horizons for actors. As the industry embraces diversity and inclusivity, Evans' commitment to authenticity and advocacy paves the way for a more inclusive future.

In a world where entertainment is a powerful force shaping cultural conversations, Chris Evans' journey becomes not just a personal narrative but a reflection of the broader shifts within the entertainment industry. As he continues to break barriers and redefine his craft, the legacy he leaves behind will undoubtedly inspire the next generation of actors to navigate the ever-unfolding adventure of lights, cameras, and action.

Beyond the silver screen, Chris Evans' influence extends into philanthropy and social impact. Engaging in charitable endeavors, he exemplifies the responsibility that comes with celebrity status. The intersection of fame and the ability to effect positive change reinforces the idea that actors can be influential advocates for meaningful causes.

Chris Evans is a prominent figure advocating for the value of inclusivity in storytelling amid the industry's struggles with issues of representation, diversity, and equality. His dedication to using his platform for good causes is indicative of a larger shift in society toward an understanding of and response to systemic problems in the entertainment industry.

As Chris Evans continues to receive attention, he is not only a gifted actor but also a representation of the significant influence that people in the public eye can have on creating a society that is more accepting and caring. In the chapters of his career that are yet to be written, the story will be interwoven with the changing dynamics of the entertainment industry and societal expectations.

Marvel's Legacy

Navigating the celebrity and obligations that accompany one's membership in the Marvel Cinematic Universe.

After portraying the legendary Steve Rogers, a.k.a. Captain America, for more than ten years, Chris Evans' Marvel legacy is woven into the very fabric of the Marvel Cinematic Universe (MCU), leaving a lasting impression on both the franchise and the superhero genre in general.

When he debuted as Captain America in "Captain America: The First Avenger" (2011), Chris Evans's career took a radical turn. His portrayal of Steve Rogers, a patriotic and principled super-soldier, won hearts and minds all over the world. As the character developed in the following movies, which included "The Avengers" (2012), "Captain America: The Winter Soldier" (2014), and "Avengers: Endgame" (2019), Evans's physical prowess was matched by his emotional nuance.

The enormous popularity of Captain America elevated Evans to a symbol of heroism both on and off-screen. Fans and fellow actors alike lauded his commitment to the role, emphasizing the responsibility that comes with representing such an iconic figure in the superhero genre. Evans confronted the unique challenge of embodying an iconic superhero while maintaining a sense of authenticity.

The pinnacle of Evans' Marvel career was reached in "Avengers: Endgame," a movie that marked both a magnificent wrap to the Infinity Saga and a heartfelt farewell for the actor, whose portrayal of Captain America's heroic and emotional journey throughout the film struck a chord with audiences and cemented Evans' legacy within the MCU.

Beyond the superhero costume, Chris Evans addressed social issues and championed causes near and dear to his heart using his platform; his involvement in social justice and philanthropic endeavors demonstrated a real-life heroism that reflected the values he portrayed on screen.

The Marvel Cinematic Universe journey of Chris Evans serves as an engaging chapter in the larger narrative of superhero cinema, leaving an enduring legacy that transcends the boundaries of the cinematic universe. Chris Evans's journey within the MCU is a testament to the enduring impact of storytelling and the ability of fictional characters to inspire real-world change, and his legacy as Captain America goes beyond a collection of box office hits.

Following the conclusion of his official run as Captain America, Chris Evans' Marvel legacy extends beyond the chronological sequence of films. His portrayal of the Star-Spangled Avengers not only contributed to the financial success of the MCU but also solidified the character's place in popular culture.

One of the remarkable aspects of Evans' tenure as Captain America lies in the character's moral complexity and emotional depth. As Steve Rogers faced personal sacrifices, confronted moral dilemmas, and grappled with the consequences of war and loss, Evans brought a nuanced performance that elevated the superhero narrative. This character complexity allowed audiences to connect with Captain America on a more profound level, transcending the typical superhero archetype.

Evans' collaboration with fellow actors, directors, and the creative team behind the MCU played a pivotal role in shaping the interconnected storytelling that became a hallmark of Marvel's success. His on-screen chemistry with co-stars, particularly his dynamic with Robert Downey Jr.'s Tony Stark/Iron Man, contributed to the emotional resonance of key moments in the MCU, such as the climactic events in "Avengers: Endgame."

Beyond the accolades and box office achievements, Chris Evans' influence on the MCU is reflected in the enduring impact of

Captain America's character arc. The mantle passed on to characters like Sam Wilson, played by Anthony Mackie, in "The Falcon and the Winter Soldier" series symbolizes a legacy that extends beyond a single actor or era.

As the MCU continues to develop, Evans' portrayal of Captain America remains an essential part of the rich tapestry of the cinematic universe, leaving an enduring legacy that will be celebrated by fans for years to come. Chris Evans' legacy as a Marvel actor is a testament to the symbiotic relationship between actor and character, transcending the boundaries of fiction to resonate with audiences globally.

Moreover, Chris Evans' influence in the Marvel Cinematic Universe goes beyond the influence of his portrayal on the larger field of superhero narratives. Under his direction, Captain America developed into a representation of optimism, tenacity, and unshakable morality—elements that went beyond the imaginary realm.

Evans' dedication to the role was evident not only in his physical transformation but also in his commitment to embodying the character's principles. Whether leading the Avengers into battle or engaging in quieter, character-defining moments, his performance added layers of humanity to the superhero genre, earning critical acclaim and endearing him to audiences of all ages.

The trajectory of ensemble superhero films was also significantly shaped by the success of Captain America during Chris Evans's tenure. The MCU's collaborative storytelling approach served as a model for other cinematic universes, influencing the way interconnected narratives unfold across multiple films and characters.

The shield and iconic imagery of the character became synonymous with Chris Evans' portrayal of Captain America, making Evans a cultural icon who transcended the realm of film to become a symbol of heroism and resilience in the collective consciousness. Evans's portrayal of Captain America left an enduring impression on popular culture and set a high bar for future superhero performances.

The evolution of Captain America in the MCU, guided by Chris Evans, serves as a testament to the power of storytelling in shaping perceptions and inspiring audiences. Whether on a solo mission or as part of the larger superhero ensemble, Captain America's legacy endures, thanks in no small part to the talent, dedication, and impact of Chris Evans on the Marvel Cinematic Universe.

Beyond the cinematic impact, Chris Evans' Marvel legacy is intertwined with the emotional resonance of his farewell in "Avengers: Endgame." The poignant passing of Captain America's shield to Sam Wilson not only marked the end of an era but also highlighted the cyclical nature of heroism and the passing of the torch. This symbolic moment showcased Evans' ability to convey a character's emotional depth and allowed the MCU to explore themes of legacy and continuity.

Evans' commitment to authenticity extended to the physical demands of the role. His rigorous training regimen and on-screen feats set a high bar for superhero portrayals, emphasizing the dedication required to bring these larger-than-life characters to life. The iconic shield throws, intense fight sequences, and moments of quiet introspection all contributed to a Captain America that was both aspirational and relatable.

As a central figure in the MCU, Chris Evans also played a crucial role in fostering camaraderie among the cast. His leadership, both on and off-screen, contributed to the chemistry that defined the Avengers as a team. The behind-the-scenes dynamics, shaped in part by Evans' approach to collaboration, added depth to the on-screen relationships, enhancing the overall storytelling experience.

Even post-Captain America, Chris Evans' influence lingers, as fans eagerly anticipate his potential return to the MCU in different capacities. The legacy of his performance continues to shape discussions about superhero narratives, character arcs, and the enduring impact of actors on the franchises they inhabit.

As the MCU develops, the echoes of Chris Evans' portrayal linger, a testament to the lasting impact of a charismatic actor who brought an iconic superhero to life in a way that will be celebrated for generations to come. In essence, Evans' legacy at Marvel is a tapestry woven with a rich blend of action-packed heroics, emotional depth, and a commitment to storytelling that extends beyond the confines of a single film.

The Hero's Heart

Chris Evans's advocacy activities and charitable endeavors.

Beyond his success on film, Chris Evans has emerged as a prominent advocate and philanthropist who uses his platform to speak out on a range of social concerns. His engagement in several initiatives shows his dedication to having a good impact:

1. **Research on kid Cancer:** Chris Evans has taken a leading role in promoting funding and awareness for studies on kid cancer. He has taken part in programs that assist young patients and their families, raising awareness of the value of financing research for pediatric malignancies via his public persona.

2. **Political Engagement:** Evans has advocated for civic duty and political involvement using his voice. On social media, he has been outspoken about his political beliefs, encouraging his

followers to vote and supporting causes that he supports. His idea that it is his duty as a celebrity to promote constructive social change is reflected in this participation.

3. **Mental Health Advocacy:** Evans has publicly shared his struggles with anxiety, acknowledging the significance of mental health. By talking about his experience, he hopes to dispel the stigma associated with mental health problems and promote candid dialogue. His openness in discussing his challenges strikes a chord with a lot of people, encouraging a positive conversation about mental health.

4. **Equality and Social Justice:** Evans has used his position to speak out against prejudice, serving as a champion for social justice and equality. He has participated in conversations on inclusiveness and diversity in the entertainment business and has shown support for initiatives to address racial inequity.

5. **Humanitarian Efforts:** Evans has been involved in several humanitarian initiatives in response to world crises. He is a shining example of someone who is dedicated to utilizing power and wealth for the benefit of society, whether he is helping with disaster relief or giving to organizations that deal with pressing issues.

6. **Environmental Conservation:** Evans has shown concern about environmental concerns and has supported programs that emphasize sustainability and conservation. His advocacy for environmental issues highlights how social and environmental responsibilities are intertwined.

7. **Veterans Support:** Chris Evans has participated in programs that assist servicemen and women in light of the sacrifices made by veterans. He has taken part in activities and partnerships with groups that support, honor, and provide resources to veterans.

8. **LGBTQ+ Advocacy:** Evans has made a strong case for inclusion and LGBTQ+ rights. He has fought for equal rights and opposed discrimination based on sexual orientation and gender identity via social media and public remarks. His position helps to create a society that is more welcoming and inclusive.

9. COVID-19 Relief Efforts: Evans participated in efforts to provide assistance and relief in response to the worldwide COVID-19 epidemic. Whether it was by boosting public health recommendations or providing funding for relief efforts, he used his power to confront the issues the epidemic presented and promote group efforts.

10. **Arts Education:** Evans has participated in programs that support young people's access to the arts and acknowledges the value of arts education. His advocacy of initiatives that foster self-expression and creativity demonstrates his faith in the transformational potential of the arts in education.

11. **Animal Welfare:** Evans has backed groups that promote animal welfare as a champion for animal rights. His endeavors include increasing consciousness on matters like the mistreatment of animals and the need for proper pet ownership.

12. **Collaboration with Charitable Organizations:** Evans has worked with several nonprofits, using his position to further their objectives. He enthusiastically supports and works with NGOs promoting good social change, whether via fundraising events, PSAs, or personal engagement.

Essentially, Chris Evans' charitable endeavors cover a broad spectrum of issues, demonstrating a dedication to making a difference on a local and worldwide level. His diverse activism demonstrates a strong sense of civic duty and a conviction in utilizing one's power to solve important problems and advance societal progress.

Chris Evans' charitable activities demonstrate the many ways in which celebrities may effect good change. Through his advocacy of several causes, he not only increases public awareness but also actively engages in endeavors to tackle urgent social issues, demonstrating a commitment to improving the world outside of the entertainment industry.

13. **Educational projects:** Evans has advocated for greater access to high-quality education and has shown a deep interest in these projects. He emphasizes the transforming role of education in forming people and communities, whether by endorsing literacy initiatives or scholarship programs.

14. **Homelessness and Housing Advocacy:** In response to the difficulties experienced by people who are homeless, Evans has offered his support to programs that aim to provide those in need with resources, support, and a place to stay. His campaign raises awareness of the intricate

problems associated with homelessness and the need to find humane solutions.

15. **COVID-19 Vaccine Awareness:** Evans has used his platform to raise awareness of the COVID-19 vaccine and urged his fans to be vaccinated in light of the international immunization campaigns against the virus. His participation in public health campaigns demonstrates his dedication to stopping the epidemic and preserving public health.

16. Crisis Response: Evans has been aggressive in advocating for assistance for impacted populations during periods of natural disasters or humanitarian crises. He demonstrates a worldwide response to pressing needs, whether via the work of relief groups or his fundraising endeavors.

17. **Anti-Bullying Campaigns:** Evans has made a strong case against bullying in general and cyberbullying in particular. His opposition to cyberbullying is in line with larger initiatives to

establish a more secure and civilized online space, stressing the value of compassion and understanding.

18. **Artistic Expression and Mental Health:** Evans has backed initiatives and programs that highlight the connection between creativity and mental health because he understands the therapeutic value of artistic expression. This is consistent with his larger support for candid discussions about mental health.

19. **Community Building:** Evans has helped his followers develop a feeling of community by interacting with them and on social media. His attempts to establish constructive online communities show a dedication to leveraging digital media for mutual assistance and constructive discourse.

20. **Worldwide Advocacy:** Chris Evans tackles problems that cut across national borders as part of his worldwide charitable reach. His support of global causes demonstrates his understanding of

the interdependence of world issues and the value of working together to find solutions.

In conclusion, Chris Evans's advocacy and philanthropy work is distinguished by its depth and breadth, covering a wide range of issues. His diverse involvement highlights a commitment to having a significant influence on the world and bringing about constructive change in sectors that align with his values and views, from social justice to healthcare, education, and beyond.

Chapter three

Love and Relationships

Insight into his connections and the balancing act of celebrity and personal life.

Chris Evans, well-recognized for his depiction of Captain America in the Marvel Cinematic Universe, has remained very secretive about his relationships despite his high-profile work. As of my latest knowledge update in January 2022, he has been engaged in a few prominent partnerships, and it's crucial to note that his personal life may have developed since then.

Evans had a well-known relationship with Jessica Biel, an actress. Between 2001 and 2006, the couple was often seen together on different occasions. However, they finally went their ways, citing clashing schedules and the limitations of sustaining a relationship in the public glare.

Following his romance with Biel, Evans has been connected to various other celebrities, including Minka Kelly and Jenny Slate. He had an intermittent connection with Kelly for a few years, and there were reports that they had many reconciliations. Evans later dated actress and comedian Jenny Slate; their public relationship, which included red-carpet appearances together, attracted attention.

Evans's personal life makes clear the difficult balancing act that must be done between retaining close ties and being well-known. There's no doubt that the intense scrutiny that comes with being a Hollywood star can affect interpersonal relationships. Evans has acknowledged the extra pressure and scrutiny that comes with being a celebrity and has occasionally discussed the difficulties of navigating relationships in the public eye.

Despite the occasional spotlight on his sexual life, Evans has typically been protective about his private relationships. He likes to keep specifics about his relationships out of the public view, preserving a degree of seclusion that contrasts with the frequently intrusive nature of celebrity culture.

It's worth mentioning that personal connections are fluid and susceptible to change, and any events in Chris Evans' personal life after my previous update in January 2022 may not be represented here. Like with any star, Evans and other people often struggle to strike a balance between their personal lives and fame, which is a difficult part of navigating the entertainment world.

Chris Evans has often underlined how important it is to keep his personal life private, even in the face of celebrity. He has mentioned in interviews that he believes it is important to keep his private life and his public persona separate, emphasizing how important it is to preserve the closeness of those relationships.

Evans's attitude to celebrity is consistent with his dedication to seclusion. He has said loudly that he would want to be acknowledged for his acting career rather than being limited by his notoriety. This viewpoint also permeates his private life, as he tries to protect important relationships from the unrelenting scrutiny that comes with being well-known.

Chris Evans is not the only celebrity who has to strike a balance between his personal life and fame; many other celebrities also struggle with the constant spotlight. Evans' deliberate attempts to conceal his connections, meanwhile, reveal a careful strategy for overcoming the difficulties that come with celebrity.

As of January 2022, when I last updated my information, Chris Evans has taken action to use his notoriety for good. He has shown a dedication to changing the world outside of entertainment by using his platform to promote several social and political concerns. This intricate component of his public character emphasizes even more how difficult it may be to have a happy, balanced life in the face of celebrity's demands.

In summary, Chris Evans' interpersonal connections and the delicate balancing act between his personal life and stardom highlight the complex aspects of being a superstar. Although he has gone through the highs and lows of well-publicized relationships, his focus on privacy and the conscious division of his personal and public lives demonstrate a methodical and thoughtful approach to overcoming the difficulties of being a well-known character in the entertainment business.

Chris Evans has dabbled with directing as a new addition to his acting repertoire. This change in emphasis has probably given him a fresh viewpoint on celebrity and how it affects one's personal life. While producing and directing have their own set of difficulties, they also offer a means of artistic expression that may not be as noticeable in one's interpersonal interactions.

While he has maintained a degree of secrecy, Evans has sometimes spoken up about his experiences and sentiments, revealing peeks into his ideas on relationships and the entertainment business. Such genuine moments give a more comprehensive view of the actor beyond his on-screen appearances.

It's vital to acknowledge that superstars, like Chris Evans, change both emotionally and professionally. The information available up to my last update in January 2022 may not capture the entirety of his experiences since then. As of that time, Evans had been candid about the impact of fame on his personal life, but specific details were often kept under wraps.

As fans and the public continue to follow Chris Evans' path, it remains to be seen how he will handle the constant balancing act of keeping a private life while prospering in the limelight. His devotion to honesty and meaningful work implies that he will continue to find methods to achieve that balance, stressing both personal satisfaction and professional success.

Chris Evans has been able to keep some privacy, but he has also welcomed social media as a way to interact with followers and disclose parts of his life at his own pace. He has been able to interact with the public and share tidbits of his personality on social media sites like Twitter thanks to his presence there. He can share glimpses into his life through this regulated mode of communication, including his opinions on different topics and behind-the-scenes photos from his projects.

Social media's development has changed the nature of celebrities by enabling direct communication between celebrities and their fan base. This gives celebrities like Chris Evans an opportunity to interact with followers while having some influence over the story that is told about his private life.

Evans's attitude to romantic relationships has changed, as seen by the general public. He has started sharing fewer things, maybe as a conscious reaction to the criticism that comes with having a public persona. This measured approach fits in with his overarching plan to strike a balance between personal boundaries and celebrity.

Chris Evans has also been involved in philanthropic endeavors, making contributions to a variety of charitable causes, as of my most recent knowledge update in January 2022. This facet of his public persona highlights his dedication to having a positive influence outside of the entertainment sector.

In summary, Chris Evans' continuous journey juggling his personal life and fame illustrates a dynamic process. Evans maintains control over his public persona while protecting aspects of his private life, whether through deliberate social media interactions, selective sharing, or participation in worthwhile projects. Fans can expect more details about the difficult balancing act he maintains as he pursues new professional opportunities and embraces various aspects of his identity.

Obstacles and Achievements

The professional and personal highs and lows, as well as the lessons discovered.

Throughout his career, Chris Evans has encountered many obstacles and victories, which have shaped his inspiring story of development and resiliency.

Difficulties:

1. **Typecasting:** Playing recognizable roles, such as Captain America, might make one susceptible to stereotypes. It has taken constant work for him to break free from the superhero stereotype and demonstrate his range as an actor.

2. Privacy vs. Celebrity Balancing Act: Evans's need for privacy has been tested by the continual scrutiny that celebrity brings, particularly in the social media era. Maintaining private connections while in the spotlight calls for some tact.

3. **Navigating Industry Pressures:** There is a lot of rivalry in the entertainment business, and there is pressure to meet standards. Evans has probably had difficulty being true to himself while also living up to industry standards.

4. **Public Scrutiny:** The public is sometimes cruel, and Evans has had to cope with gossip, conjecture, and the constant scrutiny that comes with being a well-known person. Staying true to oneself while sifting through false information is a constant struggle.

5. **Pressure of Expectations:** After successful large-scale franchises like Marvel, there is increased pressure for follow-up initiatives. For any performer, achieving and surpassing these standards without succumbing to artistic burnout may be very difficult.

6. **Handling Personal and Professional Development:** Evans has probably struggled personally to balance personal development with

a hard profession. The ongoing transformation of one's identity, values, and goals in the eyes of the public may be intimidating as well as transforming.

7. **Maintaining Work-Life Balance:** It may be difficult to strike a balance between personal well-being and hard work in the spotlight. The weight of continuously having to live up to expectations may be heavy, so finding a good work-life balance requires careful consideration.

8. **Media Sensationalism:** Handling the distorting of personal narratives and media sensationalism may be difficult. Rumors and gossip have the power to eclipse an artist's body of work, making it challenging to keep the narrative under control and the artist's accomplishments front and center.

9. **Navigating Business Changes:** Trends, technology, and audience preferences are just a few of the many changes that the entertainment business faces. It's difficult to remain relevant

and adaptive in the face of these changes; it takes constant learning and adjustment.

Achievements:

1. **Marvel Cinematic Universe Success:** One of the biggest achievements in the MCU is Evans' depiction of Captain America. His career was boosted by the success of these movies, which also demonstrated his ability to play a nuanced and endearing character.

2. **Actor Versatility:** Evans has successfully shown his variety as an actor, despite the difficulties posed by typecasting. His performances in a variety of genres, including comedy, drama, and action, show that he can play a wide range of interesting and intriguing characters.

3. **Directorial Debut:** "Before We Go," a picture that represented a personal victory, was Evans' first feature film to be directed. His decision to become a director demonstrated his desire to

broaden his creative horizons and investigate many aspects of the filmmaking process.

4. **Activist and Philanthropic Efforts:** Evans has been successful in using his platform for social and political activism in addition to his acting profession. His passion for having a constructive effect on social challenges is evident in his activism and charity.

5. **Critical Acclaim:** Evans's performances in a variety of projects have garnered praise from critics in addition to the box office success of his blockbuster movies. Acknowledgment for his acting abilities and services to the film business is evidence of his commitment and aptitude.

6. **Comradery and Professional ties:** Evans's success has been largely attributed to the good ties he has cultivated with other actors and directors in the business. Effective teamwork and a healthy work atmosphere are critical components of a successful and satisfying career.

7. **Personal Evolution:** Chris Evans has accomplished things in his life outside of his profession. His capacity to change, grow from events, and impart lessons learned about personal development adds to a real and resilient story.

8. **Fan Appreciation:** The unwavering love and support from fans all across the globe constitute a noteworthy victory. Developing a devoted following is evidence of Evans's interpersonal connections with viewers in addition to his on-screen appeal.

These continuous setbacks and victories for Chris Evans, an actor, director, and advocate, help to create a story about a multifaceted person who manages the intricacies of celebrity while adhering to his profession and values.

9. **Recognition Beyond performing:** Chris Evans's impact is acknowledged for his efforts to several causes, demonstrating that his influence

goes beyond performing. His advocacy and charitable endeavors show that it is possible to use celebrity status for good in society.

10. **Resilience in the Face of Setbacks:** Triumphs often result from handling setbacks in addition to victories. Evans's ability to overcome obstacles, grow from setbacks, and advance professionally demonstrates his fortitude in the cutthroat entertainment industry.

11. **Impact and Legacy:** Evans is leaving a lasting legacy in his roles as director, actor, and activist. His efforts for social causes and the effect his work has on viewers have created a lasting and favorable impression in the entertainment industry.

12. **Creative Exploration:** Discovering new creative undertakings might lead to triumphs. Evans' artistic quest adds dimension to his work by taking on demanding parts, experimenting with directing and participating in creative partnerships.

In summary, Chris Evans' path reflects the dynamic nature of a career in the entertainment business, as it is a tapestry weaved with both victories and setbacks. His capacity to overcome challenges and make a significant contribution to audiences and society, together with his ongoing personal and professional development, is indicative of a story of sustained success.

Chris Evans Versatility in movie industry

Chris Evans' life has been defined by a thoughtful and intentional investigation of a variety of positions in the entertainment business, even outside of his well-known role as Captain America.

1. **Various Acting Positions:** indie Films: Evans has aggressively pursued parts in indie productions, which have allowed him to work on stories that are more complex and character-driven. This change is a reflection of his desire to show off his versatility as an actor outside of high-end blockbusters.

Dramatic and Comedy Genres: By accepting parts in both dramatic and humorous genres, the actor has shown his adaptability and ability to work with a variety of narrative motifs. His careful choice of roles demonstrates his desire to push himself as an actor.

2. **directing endeavors Before We Go:** Evans's choice to direct his first film, "Before We Go," showed a dedication to artistic discovery and progress while delving into a new aspect of narrative. This step goes beyond acting and indicates a willingness to contribute to the creative process.

3. **Philanthropy and Civic Engagement:** Since leaving the cast of Captain America, Evans has taken an active part in civic and philanthropic endeavors. By using his position to promote social and political concerns, he has shown his dedication to leaving a constructive legacy outside of the entertainment sector.

4. **Counterbalancing Independent Projects with Blockbusters "Knives Out" and "Defending Jacob":** Evans's work on these two films demonstrates a way to strike a balance between big-budget entertainment and smaller-scale, character-driven stories. This balance enables him to play roles that are both

complex and nuanced while still appealing to a wide range of viewers.

5. **Self-improvement and introspection:** Public Reflections: In interviews and on social media, Evans has opened up about his personal development and thoughts on life after Captain America. This openness makes it possible for viewers to relate to him more deeply and highlights the human condition that lies beyond the glamorous exterior.

6. **Handling Public Reputation:** Measured and Selective Public Presence: Evans has continued to be active on social media, but he has taken a calculated and selective approach to his public persona. This calculated involvement enables him to communicate with followers while protecting aspects of his personal life.

By experimenting with a variety of roles, taking advantage of directing opportunities, participating in advocacy, and sharing personal reflections, Chris Evans has essentially created a post-Captain America narrative that transcends the boundaries of a superhero franchise. This purposeful and multifaceted approach positions Evans as more than just an actor, but as a creative force that makes a meaningful contribution to the entertainment industry and public discourse.

7. **Group Projects and Collaborations:** Evans has aggressively pursued partnerships with gifted actors and directors, taking part in group endeavors that highlight the industry's creative synergy and camaraderie; these kinds of collaborative endeavors add to the depth of Evans' post-Captain America career.

8. **Coaching and Developing Up-and-Coming Talent:** Outside of his work, Evans has shown a desire to mentor and assist up-and-coming artists. Whether by way of production or by standing out for underrepresented voices in the field, he adds to the story of promoting diversity and innovation.

9. **Accepting Character Complexity:** Since leaving Captain America, Evans has been drawn to complicated, ethically dubious characters. Taking on parts like "Defending Jacob" that require him to embrace complexity helps him to explore the subtleties of human nature and push himself as well as viewers.

10. **Ongoing Box Office Achievement:**
Evans has retained his box office appeal while taking on a variety of roles. His post-Marvel endeavors, such as the critically acclaimed "Knives Out," show that he can attract crowds and have an influence at the box office outside of the superhero genre.

11. **Upcoming Initiatives and Creative Projects:** Evans's upcoming endeavors span a variety of artistic disciplines and genres, demonstrating a persistent dedication to diversity in narrative. Whether he is producing, directing, or acting, he is molding a career that shuns convention and welcomes the unexpected.

12. **Worldwide Effect and Association with Fans:** Evans' career has a worldwide influence and a fan base that cuts over national and cultural divides; his capacity to engage a wide range of audiences highlights the attractiveness of his work to all audiences and his contributions to the entertainment industry worldwide.

13. **Sustaining an Authentic Feeling:** Evans has worked hard to keep his public character honest during this post-Captain America period. Whether he's sharing personal tales or offering his thoughts on social concerns, he manages to engage audiences in a manner that seems real and approachable.

Chris Evans' post-Captain America journey is marked by a purposeful and dynamic exploration of roles, genres, and creative endeavors as he continues to maneuver through the constantly changing entertainment landscape. Evans upholds his values, embraces complexity, and fosters collaboration to contribute to a narrative that transcends the shield and leaves a lasting impression on both audiences and the industry at large.

14. **Going Beyond Conventional TV and Film:** Evans has demonstrated a willingness to experiment with storytelling in media other than traditional film and television. Whether it is through his work on creative digital projects, streaming services, or emerging media, he continues to be receptive to new forms of artistic expression and demonstrates adaptability in a quickly evolving field.

15. **Promotion of the Environment:** Outside of the entertainment industry, Evans has shown a strong commitment to environmental advocacy. Along with his charitable work, his participation in campaigns centered around climate change and sustainability shows that he is willing to use his platform to effect positive change on a larger scale.

16. **Creating an Impactful Legacy:**

Evans is intent on leaving a lasting legacy as his career develops. Whether it be via lobbying, charity, or mentoring, he is actively fostering a constructive and long-lasting influence on both the entertainment sector and society as a whole.

17. A Comprehensive Strategy for Well-Being: Since leaving Captain America, Evans has been transparent about the value he places on his mental health and general well-being. His support of mental health awareness raises awareness of the significance of holistic wellbeing and feeds a bigger discourse in the industry and society.

18. International Partnerships:
Evans has embraced worldwide cooperation, collaborating with actors and directors from all over the world. This global perspective enhances his own artistic experiences and helps to create a more connected and inclusive entertainment business.

19. **How to Handle Parenthood:** Having children has probably brought another level of complication to Evans' life. His post-Captain America trajectory is multifaceted, with him juggling a successful job, personal relationships, and fatherhood.

20. **Appreciation and Lowliness:** Evans has maintained a humble demeanor in the face of success and has been grateful for the opportunity he has been given throughout his post-Captain America undertakings. This approachable demeanor makes him popular with both fans and colleagues and helps him project a good and grounded public image.

To sum up, Chris Evans' life outside of the Shield is a rich tapestry of artistic exploration, advocacy, and personal development. Through taking on a variety of projects, rising to new challenges, and actively participating in public discourse, he is creating a legacy that extends far beyond his legendary superhero role and will leave a lasting impression on both the entertainment business and society at large.

Chapter four

Chris Evans collaboration with co-stars

Chris Evans has had a prolific career spanning several decades, and he has been featured in a wide range of films across various genres. Here are some notable movies that feature Chris Evans:

1. **The actress Scarlett Johansson:** Chris Evans (Captain America) and Scarlett Johansson (Black Widow) have a strong on-screen relationship as fellow Avengers in the Marvel Cinematic Universe. Their off-screen chemistry resulted in partnerships in several promotional appearances and interviews.

2. **The actor Robert Downey Jr:** A fundamental aspect of the Avengers movie was the friendship between Chris Evans and Robert Downey Jr., who played Iron Man. Their closeness was evident via their cooperation,

which extended beyond the screen to include combined appearances in press tours, interviews, and social media exchanges.

3. **Sebastian Stan:** In the MCU, Sebastian Stan's character, Bucky Barnes (Winter Soldier), had a close bond with Captain America. Stan and Evans's connection off-screen resulted in moments of camaraderie during press conferences, creating a vibrant and interesting collaboration.

4. **Anthony Mackie:** On and off screen, Anthony Mackie, who played Sam Wilson (Falcon), developed a close relationship with Chris Evans. Their cooperation continued into interviews, highlighting their sincere relationship as well as the interplay between their personalities.

5. **Christopher Hemsworth:** During promotional engagements, Chris Evans and Chris Hemsworth displayed a warm and lighthearted interaction, reminiscent of their time

spent together as Captain America and Thor in the Avengers flicks. The ensemble cast's general chemistry was enhanced by their cooperative efforts.

6. **Mark Ruffalo:** While on Avengers press tours, Chris Evans collaborated with Mark Ruffalo (Hulk), displaying a friendship that mirrored the close-knit connections inside the MCU. Their collaborative interviews and promotional appearances emphasized the franchise's ensemble vibe.

7. **Jenny Slate:** Chris Evans was romantically associated with actress Jenny Slate before the MCU. Their partnership continued until the movie "Gifted," in which they starred as the main characters. Their collaboration provided an insight into Evans's work outside of superhero roles.

8. **Ana de Armas:** Chris Evans and Ana de Armas worked together on the movie "Knives Out." Their chemistry on screen and their

collaborative efforts in the film's marketing revealed another aspect of Evans' acting talent in a murder mystery group.

9. **Michelle Dockery:** Chris Evans worked with Michelle Dockery on the Apple TV+ series "Defending Jacob." Their collaboration on screen and combined marketing efforts emphasized Evans' entry into television and his versatility in several media.

10. **Directorial Cooperation - "Before We Go":** Chris Evans made his directing debut working with Alice Eve on the movie "Before We Go." This was a turning point in Evans' career since it was his first time directing, demonstrating his newfound ability to work with co-stars.

Chris Evans works with directors, producers, and crew people in addition to his co-stars. His capacity to forge solid professional bonds adds to the entertainment industry's spirit of cooperation and connectivity.

The Aftereffects of a Superhuman

Analyzing the long-term effects and contributions of Chris Evans to the entertainment business.

The impact of Chris Evans as a superhuman goes much beyond his role as Captain America in film. His influence is wide-ranging, affecting not just the entertainment sector but also public discourse and the lives of his devotees. The following are significant facets of his legacy:

1. **Symbol of Integrity and Heroism:** Evans' portrayal of Captain America transformed the character into an exemplar of selflessness, bravery, and integrity. His performance struck a chord with viewers throughout the world, igniting appreciation for the virtues that Captain America stands for.

2. **Enhancing the Superhero Category:** Evans' contributions to the Marvel Cinematic Universe were crucial in boosting the popularity of the superhero subgenre. His dedication to depth and realism gave the genre more gravity and helped it gain traction as a respectable narrative format.

3. **Good Effect on Fans:** Evans's encounters with fans, both in person and virtually, have had a favorable and enduring effect. Because of his sincere and personable manner, he has gained the respect and connection of admirers all around the globe.

4. **Handling Notoriety with Grace:** Evans's capacity to manage notoriety with dignity and modesty establishes a standard for how well-known people may manage the demands of media attention. Respect has been earned for his genuineness and down-to-earth demeanor in interviews and public appearances.

5. **Diversity of Roles:** Evans' career spans a wide variety of parts outside of the superhero

genre, demonstrating his flexibility as an actor. This legacy challenges industry preconceptions and typecasting by promoting a more expansive view of performers' skills.

6. **Advocacy for Social Issues:** Evans's vocal support of political and social causes has helped to establish a tradition of using celebrity power to effect good change. His endeavors to increase consciousness and engage in charitable endeavors demonstrate a dedication to effecting change outside of the entertainment industry.

7. **Collaboration and Mentoring:** Through his mentoring of up-and-coming talent and his collaborative attitude, Evans leaves a legacy of encouraging inclusiveness and originality in the business. Future generations will find him to be an inspiration because of his eagerness to work together and help others.

8. **Impact on Mental Health Discourse:** Evans' candor on difficulties with mental health and the significance of getting treatment has had a big

influence on the conversation around mental health. He helps dispel stigmas and promote dialogue about mental health by sharing his own experiences.

9. **Philanthropic Contributions:** Evans has a heritage of using his notoriety and clout to solve social concerns via his philanthropic work and support of several charity initiatives. His donations benefit underprivileged areas and issues outside of the film industry.

10. **A Durable Filmic Presence:** Through enduring characters like Captain America, moviegoers have a deep appreciation for Chris Evans' film history. He will always be honored and recognized for his important contributions to the history of film by the films in which he starred.

To sum up, Chris Evans' influence as a superhuman surpasses his involvement in superhero movies. His effect is multifaceted, including his contributions to film, his activism for social causes, his influence over fans, and his long-lasting influence on the culture and ethos of the entertainment business.

11. **Changing the Meaning of Masculinity:** The way Chris Evans plays Captain America has redefined conventional ideas of what it means to be a man. The figure defies clichés and adds to a more complex portrayal of masculinity in popular culture by embodying strength, bravery, and vulnerability.

12. **Inspiration for Future Actors:** Evans' transformation from a little-known actor to a Hollywood celebrity is an example for aspiring actors. His flexibility, devotion to meaningful narrative, and passion for his art raised the bar for others entering the field.

13. **Influence on Popular Culture:** Pop culture is infused with Evans' legacy even outside of the silver screen. Captain America's shield, catchphrases, and memorable incidents have become part of everyday culture, guaranteeing

that they will always come up in discussions about superheroes and movies.

14. **Character Evolution:** Evans' depiction of Captain America follows the character's development in the comic books. The character's path from a soldier trapped in time to the head of the Avengers illustrates themes of fortitude, flexibility, and the never-ending pursuit of justice.

15. **Determining the Success of a Franchise:** Evans' depiction of Captain America is closely linked to the Marvel Cinematic Universe's success. His captivating and deeply felt performance was a major factor in the success and praise bestowed upon the series by critics.

16. **Legacy of Family and Parenthood:** Evans has shaped narratives about striking a balance between a prominent job and personal connections as he manages family life and parenting. His dedication to privacy while being

true to himself is an example of how to keep your ordinary in the face of celebrity.

17. **Constructive Advocate**: One aspect of Evans' legacy is his advocacy for constructive change, as noted in point Whether promoting environmental concerns, social justice, or mental health awareness, he utilizes his position to draw attention to crucial topics and inspire meaningful dialogue among people.

18. **Effect on Upcoming Generations:** Future generations will continue to feel the influence of Chris Evans' legacy. Hollywood's environment is expected to change when new performers join the business because of its impact on social participation, narrative, and authenticity.

19. **Promoting a Feeling of Community:** Through his relationships with co-stars, fans, and collaborators, Evans contributes to the entertainment industry's tradition of building a feeling of camaraderie. His real connection and

approachability with others foster an atmosphere of innovation and mutual support.

20. **Humanity's Legacy:** Apart from his portrayal of superhuman characters, Chris Evans' lasting significance stems from his embodied humanity. His sincerity, kindness, and dedication to having a good influence are what make him a real-life superhero, both on and off film.

To sum up, Chris Evans left behind a rich legacy that goes beyond the confines of his job. It includes activism, personal development, cultural impact, and a long-lasting effect on the entertainment sector. This superhuman actor's legacy keeps growing and inspiring as his journey progresses.

Moral lessons from the life of Chris Evans

People from many walks of life might find inspiration and resonance in the moral lessons presented in Chris Evans's narrative.

1. **Embrace Authenticity:** Evans' dedication to being genuine both on and off screen instills the value of being loyal to oneself. A more real and satisfying existence might result from accepting and embracing your imperfections.

2. **Handle Difficulties with Resilience:** Evans exhibits tenacity in the face of obstacles in his professional life as well as the demands of celebrity. Learning to overcome failures and go on is an important lesson in overcoming the inevitable challenges that life presents.

3. **Use Influence for Positive Impact:** Evans uses his notoriety to promote environmental and social concerns. This illustrates how influence can be a potent instrument for good, inspiring

others to utilize their platforms to make a significant difference.

4. **Juggling Private and Public Life:** Evans' strategy for striking a balance between private and public appearance highlights the need to establish limits. In the era of continual connectedness, knowing how to maintain personal space while navigating the public glare is an essential skill.

5. **Growth Through Vulnerability:** Evans promotes the concept that vulnerability can be a source of strength by candidly sharing his experiences with fear and self-doubt. Expressing one's struggles to others encourages empathy and a sense of community.

6. **Examine Diverse Positions:** Evans's range of employment demonstrates the importance of welcoming variation in one's career aspirations. Personal and artistic development might result from experimenting with various roles and genres.

7. **Encourage Significant Connections:** Evans emphasizes the need to preserve deep ties while stressing the need for privacy in intimate interactions. One important moral lesson is to value connections more than one's approval from the public.

8. **Mentoring and Working Together:** As an example of raising people with you on your ascent, Evans collaborates and coaches up-and-coming talent. Promoting a collaborative and supportive culture is advantageous for both people and the business at large.

9. **Environmental Stewardship:** The moral lesson of taking responsibility for the world is highlighted by Evans' participation in environmental campaigning. It highlights the part that every individual can play in making the world more environmentally friendly and sustainable.

10. **Use Humility to Navigate Success:** Evans stays grounded and modest despite his achievements. This moral instruction exhorts people to approach success with humility as it often requires teamwork.

11. **Mental Health Advocate:** Evans helps to lessen stigma by being transparent about his difficulties with anxiety and raising awareness of mental health issues. This moral lesson highlights the need to place a high priority on mental health and create a welcoming atmosphere for those who are struggling with mental health issues.

12. **Legacy Exceeding Roles:** Beyond his on-screen personas, Evans is remembered for highlighting the moral lesson that one's influence may transcend beyond one's primary field of expertise. It is worthwhile to work toward leaving a lasting legacy and making a constructive contribution to society.

Essentially, the lessons that Chris Evans's biography teaches are those of societal duty, genuineness, resiliency, and the value of personal development. Those who are pursuing their life paths might draw inspiration from his experience.

Summary

In summary, Chris Evans's journey from a young actor overcoming the industry's obstacles to becoming a Hollywood star marks the climax of his narrative.

The significance of tenacity and persistence in the face of difficulty is one important lesson to be learned from Evans's story. Evans had obstacles and self-doubts throughout his career, but he overcame them every time, proving that perseverance and a strong work ethic are essential for success.

A noteworthy feature is Evans's dedication to self-improvement. As he developed emotionally and professionally, he accepted responsibility and made use of his position to speak out on social concerns. This emphasizes the notion that living a meaningful life is a result of self-discovery and ongoing growth.

Furthermore, Evans's choice to play Captain America, a figure associated with morality and bravery, shows his commitment to utilizing one's power for good. As the superhero he represented, this emphasizes the moral lesson of utilizing one's abilities and chances to constructively contribute to society.

The significance of authenticity is also emphasized in Chris Evans's story's ending. Even with the glitz and glamor of show business, Evans has been candid about his battles with anxiety and the demands of stardom. His readiness to expose these weaknesses inspires others to accept their flaws and fosters an environment of honesty.

Morally speaking, Evans's charitable endeavors and support of several causes, such as environmental concerns and civic involvement, highlight the importance of leveraging notoriety and wealth to change the world. This serves to support the notion that achievement ought to be paired with a feeling of obligation to the larger society.

Essentially, the biography of Chris Evans ends with a tale of development, resiliency, genuineness, and social responsibility. It offers insightful information on the values that may direct a happy and meaningful life, making it an uplifting model for others paving their pathways.

www.ingramcontent.com/pod-product-compliance
Lightning Source LLC
Chambersburg PA
CBHW050033260726
48658CB00005B/1578